One Heart Consciousness

A
Call to
Light Workers

A
Call to
Light Workers

Ignite Your Intuitive Instinct

John Corsa and Cindy Morris, MSW

One Heart Consciousness

BALBOA.
PRESS
A DIVISION OF HAY HOUSE

Cindy Morris, MSW and John Corsa
One Heart Consciousness, LLC
720. 480. 9322
Cindy@IgniteYourSoulPotential.com
http://IgniteYourSoulPotential.com

Balboa Press books may be ordered through booksellers or by contacting:
Balboa Press
A Division of Hay House
1663 Liberty Drive
Bloomington, IN 47403
www.balboapress.com
1 (877) 407-4847

Lay-out and cover design by Ian Kirkpatrick
Photos of Cindy and John by Barb Colombo, 11:11 Productions

Printed in the United States of America.

ISBN: 978-1-4525-9352-4 (sc)
ISBN: 978-1-4525-9353-1 (e)
Library of Congress Control Number: 2014903607

Balboa Press rev. date: 3/11/2014

This book is dedicated to all beings of higher consciousness
who have paved the way before us,
to all individuals of light working to bring the
One Heart Consciousness of Unconditional Love
and Unity to our planet
and to our extended family and friends
who support our work
in so many ways.

A call to Light Workers has gone out through the cosmos to herald the dawn of the new Golden Age, the awakening of the new consciousness, the consciousness of unity – the One Heart Consciousness. The time of the spiritual revolution has arrived. You, as a Light Worker awakening to the call, are a leader of the spiritual revolution.

As you awaken you are becoming aware of the vast potential of light pouring in. This light needs to be grounded into the Earth for the expansion and transformation of polarity consciousness to the consciousness of oneness, the One Heart Consciousness.

It is unrealistic to expect the world to change if you, as a human incarnation of Creator energy, do not create the changes inside yourself. To assist in the birth of the new consciousness you are being asked to change your own frequency by shedding old limiting programming, destroying outdated scripts, and learning techniques to properly ground the light, the energy of the new, into your consciousness and into the Earth.

The frequency of change has to reach the tipping point where it is no longer possible to hold on to the old ways of separation and limitation. You create the tipping point by committing to your own healing - the raising and maintaining of your own vibration - in this pivotal time of endless potential.

Step into your full potential by igniting your intuitive instinct, your personal internal navigational system. You are the way shower, the bearer and grounding force for light. The light will lead you home, to LOVE, to unity, to the One Heart Consciousness.

Table of Contents

Introduction   page 1

1. Your Intuitive Instinct   page 5

2. Ego Patrol   page 11

3. Chakras   page 21

4. Grounding   page 39

5. Psychic Boundaries   page 47

6. Analytical Mind/Intuitive Mind   page 63

7. Your Intuitive Style   page 75

8. Healing   page 85

Glossary   page 93

About the Authors   page 97

Chapter 1

Your Intuitive Instinct

Your instinct is an inborn pattern of your natural intuitive power. Your instinct, your intuition, is the most powerful tool you have for guiding you through your life. You were born with this powerful internal navigational system and then systematically taught not to use it. Instead, you were taught to turn your personal power over to external sources who would determine what is right and good for you. You could not have done anything to avoid this because you needed the approval and care of those who raised you in order for you to feel safe and accepted in a world you were too young to manage by yourself. This disempowerment was, in all likelihood, perpetrated upon you so you would "fit in" and be a part of the culture in which you were raised. Slowly, you learned to not trust yourself and to turn your own inner knowingness over to those you thought knew better than you: your parents, your friends, your spouse, your religion, your community, your government.

On some level, you knew that this did not feel right, but you were not aware that you had any other choice.

You do.

Your intuition is instinctual. Using your intuition is an instinctual process. The natural instinct to follow one's higher guidance is easily obscured by the learned, rational thought process, which is inherently limiting. To function at your full potential it is ideal to learn to combine your intuitive instinct with your rational thought process.

You can reclaim your intuition, your instinct, your unique and personal internal guidance system that connects you directly to your higher guidance, your direct connection to Source. Your intuition is a completely clean connection to Source energy, untainted by anyone else's opinion or will. Your intuitive instinct will always direct you safely and appropriately through your life. Once you learn to listen to your intuitive instinct, using proper discernment, you will learn to recognize and trust your inner voice. As you learn to listen to and follow your inner voice, you will never have to look outside yourself for validation of the truth of what is good and correct for you.

Your intuition is your cleanest barometer of any situation, the most unbiased and purest guidance that is available to you. A well-developed connection with your intuition will help you determine what are good and healthy choices for you in any situation. As you learn to trust yourself, you will be able to make decisions that are best for you, quickly and confidently. You will learn to develop and maintain appropriate mental and psychic boundaries with others so your personal, psychic space is kept clean and pristine. You will be able to assess any situation - a room you enter, a person you meet, or anything else you encounter. You will be able to use your personal energy for your benefit, choosing to whom you give it and when.

Developing and using your intuitive instinct is an ongoing process, like working a muscle in your physical body. If you do not use a muscle it will atrophy and you will no longer be able to use it. It's the same with your intuition. If you do not develop your intuitive instinct and learn to work with it, it will atrophy and you will become dependent on others to run your life for you.

Your intuitive instinct is like a river in winter. Ice might be covering the top layers of the river, but at some spots you can see the river flowing under the ice. That is how intuition is - always flowing. The ice - that which you have decided is true but may not be correct - is what you need to melt. Growing up in this world, in this society, we have been told many things about what we are unable to do, and we are told that there are gifts we could not possibly have. The rules of society have created your vision, which can easily become tunnel vision, closing you off from your instinct. Maybe you can only see a tiny speck of your intuitive gifts, or maybe you can see nothing at all of your intuition. As you begin to work with these instincts practice saying, "It is okay to know everything I need to know for myself. I can start opening doors to my abilities to perceive and know everything I need to know."

You may have been told that your intuition has no value and is useless, that having and using your psychic gifts is dangerous. You may have been falsely told that those who use such gifts are dangerous, that they are witches, magicians, or crazy people, people to be feared but not respected. Every human being has the ability to develop and effectively use their instinctual intuition as a powerful navigational tool and guide. Learning to use your intuition restores all power to you, the power you were born with, your divine birthright to discern and make decisions for yourself.

In this book you will learn specific techniques and practices to connect you with your own intuition, empowering you to live the rich and choice-filled life you were born to live, free of other people's fears and agendas that can rob you of your own free will.

Because your intuition may have been lying dormant for a very long time or may have been trying to get your attention as you looked to others for guidance, you will need to spend time every day tending to its development. Like a newborn, your intuition needs you to feed and nurture it so it can grow strong and be the most dependable and miraculous aspect of your being.

Ask your intuition questions. Wait for an answer and, if you are correct, affirm and congratulate yourself. Never shame or blame yourself if you are not correct. Try again. When you judge your abilities as being right or wrong, they diminish in strength. The more you affirm your abilities, the more they can grow. Punitive self-talk can shut down a whole part of your intuitive ability and you absolutely don't want to do that!

When a baby is learning to walk, you encourage her. If the baby falls you don't judge or scold her, you encourage her to get up and try again. So it is with your intuition. Keep practicing. No matter how many times you fall down, get back up and practice again. Eventually it will become natural, like walking. You won't even have to think about your intuition; it will be functioning fully, naturally, as a matter of course.

This book is a specific guide for light workers, healers, and intuitives. Light workers are beings who have incarnated to bring healing to the planet. Often light workers are healers themselves, but not necessarily. Light workers can be found at all levels of society and in all occupations.

Incarnating as a light worker is a choice the soul makes before it incarnates. It is not uncommon for a light worker to incarnate into families and conditions that need their light and their healing. Often the light worker cannot find connection and support within the family so he is pushed to go directly back to Source for connection. When the connection to Source is secured, he is then able to bring in the light with ease and grace. Each light worker needs to do her own personal healing and, in so doing, heals the family and the situation into which she was born and in which she lives.

It is not always easy to be a light worker, but it is a soul purpose filled with joy at the prospects of healing our beautiful planet, soul by soul by soul.

Chapter 2

Ego Patrol

You can think of your intuitive instinct as a huge dam of energy. The ego is the valve that controls the flow of that energetic dam. You can never rid yourself totally of the ego, though sometimes you might feel you want to. You need your ego to exist. You need to work with your ego so that it is maintaining exactly the correct valve control on your energetic dam.

You need to educate, soothe, and encourage your ego. The ego needs to know it will not be set aside as you develop and use your intuitive instinct, that it is still needed and has value. Practice saying to your ego, "Learning to use our intuition will be helpful to us. This is going to help us know what is good for us. This is going to help us not go into situations that are life-threatening." The ego likes to hear this because its job is to keep the integrity of life going. You need to talk to your ego, soothing its fears of annihilation.

Your ego is like a wild dog. Your intuitive awareness is your psychic baby. You need to train the wild dog not to attack and destroy your psychic baby. The ego is going to say things like, "You are not intuitive. This is ridiculous." The ego does not like change. The ego thinks it will die if there is change. The ego is primarily concerned about living, and it will try to destroy everything that it perceives as threatening to its life. The ego perceives itself as your identity, and it will do whatever it needs to do to maintain that identity, even if it means killing the psychic baby.

Coach your ego and say, "I am never going to say a negative thing about my intuition. I may say that I am not as accurate as usual, but I am continuing to work on developing my intuitive skills."

Several resistances can come up for the ego. The ego says, "I can't do this. I am not good at this." When that comes up, reaffirm your practice. Think reaffirming thoughts. Practice saying, "I am building my intuition. I am protecting my psychic baby. I am feeding and nourishing my psychic baby so it will grow." As you continue to give your intuitive instinct positive reinforcement the ego will begin to pull back its control.

The other thing the ego will probably say is, "This is crazy. You are crazy. You are making all this up." To that you need to show the ego some test results. You need to show the ego that your intuition knows a lot and that it needs the ego to help it, to keep from sabotaging it. Say to your ego, "Are you trying to sabotage us? Are you trying to make it so we are not going to be successful?" The ego will turn around for that. The ego wants to be successful. It thinks it needs to do everything by itself. Show the ego how well the intuitive instinct works while also admitting that there are lots of things in the world you don't know. This is true, of course, and allows the ego to know that it is still needed.

Think back to when people thought Earth was flat. Some people believed Earth was round and went off to prove it. Those who believed it was flat thought they were mad and would fall off the edge. This is continuously happening in our lives. We adamantly hold on to a thought as if it were true until proven otherwise. Your intuition, your higher guidance, gives you another thought, which you can then test, affirming as true or not true.

As with all learning, expect a learning curve. As you learn new things, the ego - which thinks it already knows everything - has to be shown that the new information is correct. Then it will adjust to the next level of mastery. Remember when you could not tie your own shoes or cook a meal for yourself? You had to work with your ego and allow for learning.

The ego is constantly present, making a valve for your own dam of energy, which is huge life force energy, while your intuition works to create more energy. If your ego is not at the right calibration for the energy to be expressed, you can have some problems. Treat your ego like a child. Be vigilant and diligent with it. Tell your ego what you need it to do to support your entire being, of which the ego is a valuable, manageable part.

Each person has a unique flow of energy, a unique relationship with the ego and the intuitive instinct. You have to work with these relationships within yourself. Affirm every intuitive hit that is correct. If an intuitive hit is not correct, not to worry, just keep trying. Do not blame or shame yourself. Keep moving forward as you practice using your intuition.

Sometimes you will receive guidance and your ego will veto the information or argue with the guidance. When that happens, your ego patrol needs to be called in to clarify that Higher Guidance is always to be followed over the ego's call. Sometimes you have no idea why Higher Guidance is directing you a certain way but when you follow the guidance you will find out and often the results are wonderful beyond belief.

As you affirm each correct intuitive feeling, your intuitive awareness and your psychic baby will continue to grow. As your psychic awareness grows, you will be able to receive more and more cues. A cue can be a feeling in your intuitive body, something you see in your mind, or something you hear with your internal sense of hearing. Continuously reaffirm your intuitive energy until it grows stronger and stronger.

You have to remain vigilant with your ego. Tell it what you want it to do and what you don't want it to do. Pay no attention to its babbling and rambling. It's just your ego. Let it continue to talk. There is no need to stop it. As you continue to soothe and coach your ego, it will find its appropriate level, the valve calibrated correctly for your needs and your intuitive development.

Each time you find your intuition is correct practice saying, "I am so amazed by my intuition and how incredibly gifted I am." Really give that statement some force.

Your ego will probably say, "What nonsense! You are not gifted! You are crazy!"

Ignore it and again affirm, "I am gifted. I am intuitive."

Every time you affirm your intuition you are feeding

and nurturing your psychic baby, which will grow bigger and stronger.

Coming Up Against Your Own Resistance

As you develop and grow your intuitive abilities, you will come up against your own resistance and your own programming. It is natural to have resistance to what is new, to what is different. Your mind will tell you, "This doesn't work. This isn't right. This is wrong." That's the ego speaking, defending its stance of staying in the familiar.

Your natural inclination is to debunk new ideas because if these new ideas are true, you will have to rearrange your entire understanding of how things work. You are coming up against your own resistance.

When you focus your mind on a single-minded understanding - on one thought or on an intuitive knowing - you increase your power to manifest, to bring that thought, that knowing, to fruition. Focus can help shift resistance to positive action.

Let's say you decide you want to run a marathon. Your ego tells you that this is truly a crazy idea. But you focus because you want to do a marathon. You keep focusing and practicing, focusing and practicing, and then you are running the marathon. That was focus and attention in action.

As humans, we have received a lot of mixed messages

about power. We have been told that having too much power is shameful, that too much power can bring death. On the other hand, we respect people in positions of power and probably want power for ourselves. Perhaps you have been told that if you are empowered, someone else will attempt to take your power away from you, perhaps even in a public setting. Perhaps a family member or a friend will vie with you for power. Sometimes it is a random stranger, volleying for position on line at the grocery store or at the gas station. Power struggles and power plays are part of our human experience

This is why it is critically important to affirm your intuition, to realize that all you are doing as you work your practices is focusing and reclaiming your personal power. You are not allowing yourself to become distracted, thereby giving your power away.

Each person has their own experience of resistance. It always comes down to whether it is okay and safe to be powerful. Remember, if the ego feels threatened and your personal safety comes into question, there will be resistance to claiming your power. As you learn to work with and trust your intuitive instinct, you will learn to follow your own guidance, not what someone else tells you. You will make decisions based on information received through your intuitive instinct, connecting your life purpose with your own life plan. As you do this more and more, you will be mastering your focus of attention, connecting to your own personal power. Claiming your own power is fueled and fed by increasing your intuitive abilities, which will naturally decrease resistance to new information coming in.

Confidence and Self-worth

The more frightened and threatened the ego becomes, the more the ego will fret away at your confidence and feelings of self-worth. When you experience a lack of confidence and lack of self-worth, you get to experience how to build yourself up. You get to experience the truth of who you really are. The ego is like a bully. The only thing a bully understands and responds to is strength. As you build confidence in your intuitive skills, you become stronger. Then you are able to stand up to the bully, your ego.

Each of us is an expression of Source energy, which has created the universe and has created each of us. The veil of unworthiness allows us to experience the challenge of feeling lack and overcoming it. It ultimately opens us to experiencing the challenge of life itself, which is growth.

From an energetic perspective, confidence is centered awareness inside you. It is not looking outside yourself for approval or acceptance. Confidence is having the strong, energetic stability that says, "I am perfect, just as I am. I am Source energy and I am continuing to work on knowing this."

For most people, understanding who they are and what they expect of themselves is more challenging than understanding and managing the world's expectations of them. It is really your interpretation of yourself and what you are lacking or what you are trying to achieve to be the best human being you can be that causes the difficulty. Your interpretation may be governed by the conditions of those around you, but they are presented through the filter of your mind, through your sense of self.

When you expand your perspective of who you are by remembering that you are Source energy and accepting yourself where you are at, then you can go from there and develop a healthy, energetic sense of self-worth.

As on a ladder, you will be able to ascend one step at a time. Have you ever climbed up a sixteen-foot extension ladder? It can be pretty scary. As you ascend it, you may fear you are going to fall. As you continue to step up the ladder of clearing energy, this same sense of fear can arise. This is the fear of your own power, of being able to trust that you are actually able to hold that energy inside of you. Each individual's process is unique. Know that you are exactly where you should be, because that is where you are.

Pandora's Box

Sometimes when you begin to delve into your intuition it can feel like Pandora's box, and if you open it up, you may fear you will not be able to manage or control all that will come out. It is natural to be cautious of what you have yet to experience. Your intuition has its own unique expression, just as you (the visible part of you walking around) have your own unique expression. Part of the caution and fear comes from your ego saying, "If you open all this up, it will be dangerous. We could go crazy. People will think we are weird, different. We could die!"

As you start to work with and develop your intuition, always remember to consciously choose those with whom you share your experiences. Share with those who are already working with their intuition. That way you won't have to be concerned that you will be considered odd or strange. This will soothe and comfort your ego, which is afraid to be judged. Look for your community, one in which you feel safe and comfortable about sharing your experiences.

As your intuition develops and you have access to more and more gifts, your ego will continue to tell you that what you are doing is scary and dangerous. You need to coach your ego to be the correct size in order to bring through all the beautiful energy that wants to come through. Tell your ego that this spiritual information is going to make you happier, that it will make your life better.

Fear comes up because you have great ability. It can be very challenging to reach out and connect with what you are most talented at, especially if your gifts are not supported by your family, your culture, and your society. Your gifts are needed! It is a fun challenge to embrace your gifts every day. The more you are afraid of opening the Pandora's box of your gifts, the greater are your gifts. Get support by staying connected with like-minded students as you develop your intuitive instinct.

Chapter 3

Chakras

The word "chakra" comes from the Sanskrit word cakra, meaning wheel or disk. The chakra system is a system of seven major energy centers in the body that regulate the flow of energy within the body and within your life. The chakras are wheels of spinning energy radiating out in all directions. Each chakra is three-dimensional. Some people see the chakras as cone-shaped, with the energy from these cones radiating out to the front and to the back, creating a vortex of energy. Others describe chakras as spinning wheels of light.

Each chakra has its own innate intelligence. As you come to understand the intelligence of each chakra, you come to learn about yourself. You will notice that you tend to "live" in certain chakras while experiencing less from others.

If a chakra is overactive or sluggish and underactive, the system is not functioning at its maximum potential. Chakra clearings and chakra balancing techniques can be learned and implemented to keep the system functioning well.

Everything that is written about chakras should be taken as advice. You will connect with your own chakras and develop your own experience with them. You may see your chakras as different colors than the colors others associate with them. You may experience them in ways other than how others experience them. That is fine. As you work with intuitive and energetic knowledge, run the information through the filter of your own intuition. The most important thing is that you are connecting to your chakras, not what you are labeling them, and certainly not what someone else labels them. Keep checking in with yourself to determine if what you are learning about your chakras is true and correct for you.

Individual Chakras

The first three chakras govern the physical body. The fourth chakra, the heart chakra, is the energetic center of the body. The fifth, sixth, and seventh chakras govern more of the outer energy - the astral realms, higher vibrational connections to angels, spirit guides, and non-physical energies.

Each chakra group needs to communicate with the others in an integrated flow of life force energy. All parts need to work together harmoniously or you will feel unbalanced, unwell, depleted of energy.

First Chakra

The first chakra is located at the base of your spine. It is red. The first chakra is the base of grounding and security, feeling comfortable in the physical body, and having vitality and strength within your body. A healthy first chakra supports physical strength, vitality, and security in the physical body. As this chakra activates, it emanates strength and security into every cell of your body and out into your aura.

If the first chakra is too big, the result can be an aggressive nature, egotistical energy, and a feeling of being deprived, which leads to an ongoing sense of needing and wanting. First chakra relationships have a feeling of survival about them. If there is an inappropriate connection with another person through the first chakra, as sometimes happens in relationships, one of the people may feel that their survival depends on the other person, or that they need to survive over the other person, or that the other person is taking away their survival.

When the first chakra is dim you feel meek, could have health issues, and may feel anxious about your own ability to survive. Your life force energy may be low, or you may be ungrounded, flighty, and scattered.

Second Chakra

The second chakra is located below the belly button at the sacrum. This chakra is orange. The main aspects of the second chakra are comfort, sweetness, and joy. This chakra supports the sexual organs, the bladder, the womb, the sacral nerve, and the kidneys. The second chakra deals with emotions, your connections to other people, the beginnings of your emotional responses to outside forces, and how you feel about your internal systems.

With a healthy second chakra you will feel happy, joyful, satiated, able to give and receive comfort and joy. You are open to your artistic and other creative abilities, you feel emotionally content, and you experience healthy expression of your sexuality.

If the second chakra is too dim, you may have the uncomfortable feeling of not allowing joy in your body and in your life. You may have strict regimentation in your life, which does not allow for free-flowing happiness and comfort in the energetic and physical bodies.

If the second chakra is too large or overly developed, you may desire grandiose indulgence, like really loving comfort foods or indulging in what comforts, which can sometimes turn into substance abuse or craving another person rather than craving yourself.

If you feel cravings for another person or become obsessed with someone, there can be inappropriate bonding and connection. This can happen as you usurp someone else's energy and not grab on to your own personal energy.

The second chakra is also one of the two chakras related to will. This will be covered in the discussion about the third chakra.

Third Chakra

The third chakra is yellow and is located at the solar plexus. This is the power or will chakra, the gem of the chakras. The third chakra governs the digestive organs and systems, the authority muscle groups, the immune system, and the nervous system.

The third chakra is one of the will centers. The second chakra is the other will center. The second and third chakras together form the will of the personality self - how you present yourself to the world and how the world perceives you and your power.

There are two types of will. There is willpower - strength and success in life. This will is located in the third chakra. The will of your whole self, your inner self, your intuitive self, the willpower that manifests and creates duality, is located in the second chakra. The second chakra births and manifests. The third chakra exerts power over something or someone.

Astral projections begin in the third chakra. If you are learning to astral project you will begin in this chakra. Many healers use the third chakra as an energy connecting point.

Your healthy third chakra feels bright and confident. You have the ability to give of yourself with no fear of being manipulated or depleted by others. You feel comfortable expressing and using your power.

A dim third chakra often correlates to a soul agreement made with a parent or other authority figure to be in less than your full empowerment so as not to threaten their power. Perhaps, as part of your soul agreement, you agreed to give away your power over many lifetimes so you could experience how to take it back. Or perhaps you have had some very powerful lifetimes in which you abused power and chose to have a lifetime with less power this time around.

If the third chakra is blown out, fuzzy, or too dominant because you are insecure or lacking in personal power, you may hold on to the energy of this chakra to compensate for what you feel you are lacking. You might build this energy up so no one will succeed it, even though you continue to feel insecure and uncomfortable with your power. If this is the case, you need to look at your own sense of personal power and ask yourself if your personal power is aligned with your soul empowerment, with your divine self or your divine will.

People who have nervous disorders can have overdeveloped or erratic third chakras.

Fourth Chakra

The fourth chakra is located at the center of the chest, at the heart. The heart chakra is green. There can be some pink mixed in there as well. The main aspect of this chakra is love and love relationships. Emotional feelings in relationships are more connected to the second chakra. Love relationships with family and friends are governed by the fourth chakra. The heart chakra supports unconditional love. Unconditional love is an

exuberant understanding of joy, peace, and personal acceptance of self and others. Unconditional love infuses the entire
system with bliss.

The heart chakra governs the cardiac nerve plexus, the
respiratory system, the cardiac system, and thymus gland.

When you are learning to do psychic readings, read from
the heart chakra.

A healthy heart chakra is able to give and receive love, to
be compassionate and non-judgment, heart-centered, warm,
and giving. A healthy fourth chakra emanates a vibrant energy
of unconditional love.

If the heart chakra is dim you feel closed off to love, fearful, reclusive, emotionally withdrawn and cold.

The heart chakra can never be too big, though it can be
unfocused or scattered. If your heart chakra feels unfocused,
you can begin to open it bigger and bigger. If your heart chakra
is already big, make sure that you are keeping it safe by grounding yourself frequently during the day and protecting it by surrounding it with light.

Ask yourself if you have given your heart chakra enough
love today. Have you let your heart chakra bloom and blossom,
or, if it has felt too open, have you told it to close down because
you no longer feel safe? Perhaps you were taught to keep your
heart closed and you don't even know how powerful an open
heart can be. If so, experiment with opening your heart a little
bit at a time.

Fifth Chakra

The fifth chakra is located at the throat and is blue. This chakra deals with communication and self-expression. The fifth chakra rules the vocal chords, the mouth, the throat, the ears, and both the thyroid and parathyroid glands.

The second and fifth chakras correspond strongly with one another. You may technically be an excellent communicator but if you feel closed down in your second chakra, you won't be putting your message across with your will. Conversely, if your will is too strong, it can negatively affect your ability to communicate effectively.

The fifth chakra is important to self-expression - how you express yourself to your friends, your family, and the world.

In many people the fifth chakra is dim, manifesting as the inability to say what they need and want to say. A dim fifth chakra can lead to frustration and a feeling of powerlessness. The person will be meek in expression, lacking in creativity. This can also look like coldness or reclusive, hermit-like behavior.

A very loud or angry person often has an overdeveloped fifth chakra. This person can be experienced as authoritarian, speak over other people, and interrupt. They may have inappropriate social boundaries and perhaps even speak offensively.

You feel a cooling or widening of the throat when you release debris from the fifth chakra. If your throat feels tense or obstructed, the sense of "having a frog in your throat", you might have experienced trauma in this chakra, either in this life or in past lives. As this trauma is cleared from the fifth chakra, full creative self-expression is allowed.

When the fifth chakra is open, full, and cleared, the person is able to express themselves, their personal creative voice is allowed expression. Creativity is not just about painting or drawing, but includes any type of creating you bring forth in the world. See how love is created in the world, how divine empowerment is created. These too are creative expressions. This correlates with the third chakra and the heart chakra. You can begin to see how the chakras work together.

Sixth Chakra

The sixth chakra is located between the brows and is the color indigo. The main aspect of this chakra is perception and self-realization. The sixth chakra deals with the medulla plexus, the pituitary gland, and the eyes. Self-realization is connected to developing your intuition and your instinctual wisdom. You can connect to the angelic realm and friends in spirit through the sixth chakra. When you connect to your sixth chakra you can release energy that is not for your highest good, allowing the energy to recalibrate at the perfect vibration. This is how you develop self-mastery.

You don't want your sixth chakra to be too blown out or too big, too forward in your head or too back. Part of self-realization is to understand that this chakra is one of the centers in you that is a strong manifestor. What you see in your imagination, what you see in your third eye (the sixth chakra), is what you can create. This chakra engages your psychic awareness, your intuitive awareness, and your ability to create your reality.

If the sixth chakra is dim you feel dull, slow, confused, foggy, unclear and unfocused.

If the sixth chakra is overdeveloped you will interrogate other people, probing into their psychic space. You will have inappropriate psychic boundaries and feel ungrounded.

It is vitally important to keep this chakra clear, making it the perfect vibration for you. The sixth chakra should be in the center of your head. Experience yourself in this chakra feeling safe, connected to guidance, and connected to your real intuitive instinct. You can use the sixth chakra to imagine and create what you want. By placing direct focus into this chakra, you can change the energy fields inside you, thus changing the energy fields outside your body.

Seventh Chakra

The seventh chakra is at the top of your head and is known as the crown chakra. The main aspect of this chakra is spirituality, Universal Source energy, and connection to all that is. It is connected to the upper skull, the cerebral cortex, and the pineal gland. This chakra is violet, white, or gold. You can also think of this chakra as ultra-violet-gold.

When the seventh chakra is healthy and functioning well you feel connected to the Divine and to the earth - you feel spiritually alive and grounded. You feel balanced and aligned with guidance from your higher guidance and from the earth.

When the seventh chakra is dim you feel separate from Spirit, disconnected from Source, burdened. You can feel a loss of connection, a crisis of faith.

An overdeveloped seventh chakra can lead to patterns of over-giving and over-caretaking of others. You're giving so much to others but you neglect to care for your own needs. In extreme cases an overdeveloped seventh chakra can lead to psychosis.

When you open up this chakra and feel divinely connected to Source, you feel healing throughout your entire body. This feeling may be subtle at first, and if you do not fully feel it, there may be blocks present. For instance, if you grew up in a religious household, you may have had some spiritual blocks placed on you that have left you with the message that you are not spiritual if you behave outside the rules and parameters of that religion, or you are not connected to Source unless you think in a proscribed way. To rid yourself of those preconditions, ask your angels and guides to dispose of those blockages.

Earth Star Chakra

The Earth Star chakra is located 12-18 inches below your feet. This chakra connects you with the deeper energy of the earth. When you place your consciousness in this chakra you can feel your grounding strongly. When you are doing energy healing work, use the Earth Star chakra to maintain your center and to ground and balance clients whose energy is concentrated in the higher chakras.

Star Soul Chakra

The Star Soul chakra is located 12-18 inches above the head. This chakra connects you to your Higher Self and universal celestial energies. Go to this chakra to access clear, intuitive guidance, to access your personal channel to higher guidance.

Working with Chakras

Some practitioners begin at the root chakra and work their way up the system. This is the Vedic system. If you are beginning at the root chakra, you want to bring in some celestial light as protection and also ground that energy into the earth. If you begin at the crown chakra, you want to ground into the earth. Always remember to ground yourself when you are doing any energetic work.

To work with a chakra, connect with the feeling of it, the strong vital life force energy of it. Allow that chakra to spin and open. Feel into the chakra. Is it too dim, lacking in vital energy? Is it too bright and overactive? If the chakra condition is unbalanced - too dim or too active - clear debris from the chakra to restore balance and harmony to the system.

Your chakras will automatically close if they are feeling unsafe. You can trust your chakras to open up to the correct energy and close down if they are not feeling safe. If there is any kind of debris in the back of the heart chakra, like old wounds that have not been healed (most often stemming from childhood wounding), blockages to love and self-love will be present, as well as blockages to receiving unconditional love.

There can also be chakra blockages that formed in past lives. The soul also brings lineages of experience, in which there can be generations of wounding. Be open to experiencing things from other lifetimes, knowing that there is great healing that can be done within your own life today by clearing the chakras, by clearing and strengthening your energetic field, and by developing your own awareness.

One of our clients, Peter, doesn't drive a car. Peter remembers being in a fatal motorcycle accident in a past life. He acknowledges this experience and still feels it in this life. He does not judge himself but he does see this is an area that could be healed. First the experience, the karmic soul memory, needs to be released, after which more understanding of the self becomes available.

Chakra Clearing

You need to keep your chakras clear, clean, and bright. To clear stagnant energy out of the aura and the body, bring down your grounding cord into the earth where the energy can be transformed. Put your attention on the specific chakra you are working with to clear it. See that chakra spinning. As you see the chakra spinning, see debris and gunk being cleared away, like a counter cleared of clutter. As you visualize debris being cleared from the chakra, see the chakra spinning clear and bright.

When you check in with a chakra and you are able to identify blocks, release them. Call on your angels, guides, and the energies of your highest good. Ask them to help you release blocks. Your angels are always there, ready to assist you at any time, for any request you have. Angels are non-interfering in that they will not intervene unless you request their help. As soon as you ask, they will help. You have to ask!

You may have a wide range of experiences while you are working with your chakras. As you work with your chakras and come to understand where the awareness of each chakra is, the intelligence of each chakra, you will come to understand how to use that awareness and energy in your everyday life. You can begin to practice using the different chakras to heal yourself. You can use the different chakra vibrations to enhance energies that are too dim and to soften energies that are too bright.

Know that whatever you experience, see, and feel as you work with your chakras is true and correct for you. If you see brown in your first chakra but you think it is supposed to be red, experience it as it is for you, without judgment. Know that it is brown for you. Each person's experience of their chakras is unique to them; your experience of your chakras is unique to you. As you develop your relationship with your chakras, your experience of them will evolve and grow, at your own pace.

Sometimes there will be a stubborn blockage in one or more of the chakras. A wound, from this life or other life-times, can be lodged in there. No blockage is too difficult to be cleared. Know that. Stuck energy can be moved by the alchemical process of transmutation. The blocked energy can be transmuted into love and healing energy. This transmutation can be facilitated with angelic help. Ask your angels for help by saying, "Angels of the highest good who work with me, I ask you to remove the blockages from (the specific chakra or chakras). Take these blockages out of my body and aura and place them in a healing bath of Source light so this energy can be transmuted into healing energy for the earth, love energy for me, or healing energy for this chakra."

You might have chakras that will require repeated clear-ings and time to fully clear. This clearing is going to take focused attention and work. Perhaps the reason that energetic debris is present and is challenging to release is for you to receive messages and   receive lessons your soul has come to learn. Do not judge or be angry about these blockages. See them as opportunities for you to learn to work on releasing stuck energy. Nothing more. Don't put a whole story on the process.

You will probably have chakras that repeatedly hold blockages and are dimmer than the others. You will have to work more with these chakras. Practice beaming from these chakras to strengthen them. The more you use each chakra the stronger the chakras will become.

Beaming from the Chakras

To beam from a chakra, focus on that chakra's energy and direct that energy from that chakra to a specific location or person. It will feel like you are lit up, expanding out from that specific chakra and that area of your body. It will feel invigorating and life-giving. If it feels draining, you are not grounded and you are not connected to Source. If you are not connected to Source, you are depleting your own energy. The goal is to be a channel for Source energy, constantly connected, as if you have personal Wi-Fi connected to Source, wherever you go.

Beaming Practice

Connect with your chakras and begin to beam from different chakras and experience how that feels. Beam from your first chakra, which is red or any color you connect with it. Feel your first chakra in your body. Feel the energy of that chakra.

Now beam from your second chakra, which is orange and is located at the base of your sacrum. Feel this chakra in your belly and in your body. Experience how the energy feels in the second chakra.

Now beam from your third chakra, which is yellow and is located at your solar plexus. How does your body feel at this chakra?

Now go to your fourth chakra, the heart chakra. The heart chakra is green and is located in the center of your chest. Beam from the heart chakra. How does this feel?

Now beam from the fifth chakra, which is blue and is located in the throat area. Experience how the energy feels at this chakra. Feel the energy at your throat and throughout your body.

Now go to your sixth chakra at your forehead. This chakra is indigo blue. Beam from this chakra and experience how the energy feels.

Now come to your seventh chakra at the top of your head. This chakra is golden violet-white. Beam from this chakra. Experience how the energy feels at this chakra. Note how your body feels at this chakra.

Beaming from the chakras is a subtle energy practice. Continue to practice and you will get better and better at beaming. When you begin to learn about the chakras, it is like exploring a cave that is new to you. No one else has looked into this cave except you.

Practice beaming from specific chakras as you interact with friends, family, and even strangers. Practice beaming from your different chakras and watch people's reactions. The next time you are at the grocery store, beam from your heart chakra and watch the cashier melt and start to talk with you. Beam from your power chakra, asserting your power in an authentic and gentle way. Watch how you use your chakras to achieve what you want in this life. Becoming more aware of your chakras and how you use them will empower and delight you.

Chapter 4

Grounding

Grounding is the single most important practice you need to do to work with your intuition. Grounding centers you, allowing a pathway for your Higher Self, your intuitive instinct, to connect with you. Every time you ground yourself you align with the stabilizing energy of Earth, anchoring you calmly and safely to your unique connection to Earth and Source. When you are stabilized and connected, the energy can flow easily from Source to your Higher Self and then into your conscious awareness. Grounding helps you create and maintain healthy psychic boundaries (which we discuss in detail in Chapter 5).

The purpose of grounding and centering yourself is to align your energies with the earth. When you are aligned with Earth's energies you can receive Source energy from the earth and release negative energy into the earth to be transmuted.

Think of grounding as plugging in to the rejuvenating, replenishing, limitless energy of Source. You know when you go to heat up some food in your toaster oven, the plug needs to be connected to a working socket that supplies electricity. If the socket is not connected to the main electric grid and/ or if the plug is not plugged in to an active connection, you'll get no juice and that food will stay as cold as when you first put it in the toaster oven. Trying to connect to your intuition without grounding first is like trying to heat up your food in an unplugged, unconnected toaster oven.

Before you do any grounding, concentrate on your breathing. Breathe calmly in and out through your nose. Practice saying to yourself, "I am here. I am doing this grounding. I am in control."

As you learn to ground and center you will learn to do this quite quickly. You can ground yourself on a busy city street, in line at a grocery store, in your car, in an airplane - anywhere at all. As you are learning to ground yourself, give yourself enough private time to fully experience the grounding. Learn to feel what it feels like to be grounded and centered in your body. When you are grounded you will feel calm and relaxed.

Grounding and visualization take time to master. Give yourself that time. Practice often. Do not feel frustrated with yourself if you feel that it is hard to focus long enough to ground yourself. At first it will take longer to clear out all negative energy and to feel like all clear energy is securely in your body.

The more you ground, the more your brain remembers how to ground and the easier and faster you will be able to center and ground.

Methods for Grounding

There are several ways to ground. Try the various methods and practice with the ones that feel most comfortable for you. Eventually you will naturally align with a method that works most effectively for you. There is no right or wrong way to ground. Whatever works for you is the correct grounding method for you.

Method # 1: Visualize a Grounding Cord

Before you begin this grounding process, open the first chakra by seeing it begin to spin at the base of your tailbone. See the first chakra as a glowing red light radiating out into your body and further out into your aura.

Visualize a grounding cord at the base of your tailbone, at the first chakra you have opened. You can use the image of the trunk of a giant redwood tree or a giant oak. Imagine the trunk coming from the base of your tailbone going all the way through the earth, into its very core. As you connect to the earth in that way you may feel an energetic tug.

Take all energy that is not of your highest good, or any discordant feelings, and let them fall down the grounding cord. You might see pictures of things and thoughts falling down the grounding cord. Say, "Whatever is not of my highest good is released from my body and my aura to drop down the grounding cord."

You can use any other natural substance, like vines or tree roots. You could also visualize a granite stone cylinder. Use something natural and solid. Water images are not good for grounding because they are fluid, not stable. You want to visualize your grounding cord as something stable and solid from Earth, like plants or stone.

Method #2: Connecting with your Will center

The will center is located four inches below your belly button. This area is a power and will center in your body. You can ground yourself by concentrating your energy at your will center.

Focus your energy at your will center and say, "I am connecting celestial and Earth energy with my will. My will lives in my will center. I am awakening and centering my will to receive and store celestial and Earth energy."

Releasing Unwanted Energies

Whichever technique works for you, know that you are connecting to either Earth or celestial energy. When you ground and center yourself, you are going to feel any energy that you have picked up or any energy that is not of your highest good.

Those energies are to be released. Visualize the energies to be released as grey or dark spots leaving your body and auric field. As you push unwanted energy out, see it either dropping down into the earth or being taken away and out into space. Say, "Any energy that is not of my highest good I am releasing now through grounding myself."

If you have specific angels or spirit guides, or if you receive direct guidance you enjoy working with, say to them, "I would like you to take this energy away." Archangel Michael is a powerful archangel of protection and clearing. If you feel drawn to call on him say, "Archangel Michael, take away all energy that is not of my highest good."

Bringing in Healing Energy

However you choose to remove negative energy, visualize the energy being cleared from your body and aura. After the unwanted energy is cleared there is room to bring in helpful, healing energy. Think of a full refrigerator that has old food in it. Before you bring in new fresh food you want to clear out the old. When the old food is tossed and the shelves are cleaned, the new fresh food you bring will nurture and support you. Energy in your body and aura works the same way. Clear out the old crap, clean the space, and now you are ready to bring in healing, supportive energy.

There are several ways to bring in extra healing energy. If you are connecting to the earth with a healing cord, see that energy being transmuted by the earth into healing energy. Leave some energy as an offering of thanks to the earth. Visualize that energy coming back up the grounding cord, coming up through the root chakra, into your seat and legs, and continuing to travel through your body.

If you are grounding through the will center bring healing energy in from above or from all around you. See beautiful shooting stars directing life force energy and light to your will center. As each star connects to the will center it grows bigger. See this beautiful life force energy grow so big that it encompasses your entire body and aura. Visualize yourself grounding that energy into the core of the earth. For extra grounding visualize roots of light with your grounding cord.

If you are bringing healing energy in from above direct it down into Earth to offer healing to it.

After you have brought in the light or brought in the healing energy from the earth, bring your energy in close to you so you don't remain too wide open. Grounding is centering and protecting. As you ground you will naturally start to bring your energy in close around you. You don't want your energy to be too "out there," like an out-of-focus camera, creating a fuzzy image. You want to bring your energy into focus. Bring your energy in to you so it feels like it is vibrating around you. As your energy vibrates around you you will more easily be able to connect with it.

Grounding Other People

Grounding is one energetic practice you can do for other people because it supports them. When you ground another person you are saying, "I am going to give you a foundation to run your energy and send protective light your way." Grounding another person is not healing them. You can only heal another person if you ask their permission.

Before you ground another person, ground yourself first. It's like when you are on an airplane and you are instructed that, in the event that oxygen is needed, you are to put your own oxygen mask on first before you try to help someone else. Ground yourself first before you attempt to ground anyone else.

Techniques for Grounding Another Person

Tree trunks

See a large, stable tree trunk with supportive roots reaching down into the earth and, as you are focusing on the other person, say, "You are on Earth. You are here to do a mission. I support the mission you are here to do and I support your healing." Connect that person's energy to Earth. Feel them as solidly connected.

Column of Light

Surround the person with the pink light of self-love. The greatest gift you can give another person is the gift of loving themselves. When you love yourself completely you are open to all the *love* the universe has to give you, veering you away from any harm doing to yourself or others.

You can *always* help and support other people by radiating your own bright light and allowing others to experience your joy and light. Simply being bright, filling yourself with love, affects others in a positive, uplifting way.

How Often to Ground

It is important to ground and center yourself daily. Set times during the day to do your grounding. Do your grounding practice as many times a day as you would like. If you find yourself in stressful situations you can ground yourself more frequently, as often as you like. Grounding yourself frequently during the day keeps you connected to Source energy and keeps your energy clear of debris. The more you ground and center yourself the more relaxed you will feel.

Chapter 5

Psychic Boundaries

It is critical for you to maintain healthy psychic boundaries, not only when you are working with your intuition, but every moment of every day of your life here on Earth. Creating and maintaining healthy psychic boundaries keeps your energetic body clear, free of other people's agendas, opinions, and psychic debris. Keeping your psychic boundaries clean and clear will prevent the development and growth of serious behavioral disease patterns like codependence, over-giving, self-sacrifice, and believing in self-limiting, false self-titles. These dysfunctional behaviors are as serious as cancer and can be just as debilitating. The clearer you keep your energetic field and the healthier your psychic boundaries, the happier and healthier a person you will be.

As you walk around in your everyday life, energy is flowing and moving around you constantly. In each conversation and interaction you have, you are bouncing energy back and forth, exchanging energy with others. Any thoughts you entertain also bring energy into you. All experiences you have bring energy in to you.   Let's say you happen to walk past someone in the grocery store and he gives you a nasty look. Perhaps he simply isn't happy that day and has decided to energetically toss his unhappiness your way. Actually, he may not have even made a conscious decision to behave this way.

Energy can come towards you as a net or a spurt. If your energy field is wide open, if your psychic boundaries are not appropriately intact, you will take that energy on, perhaps without even knowing you are doing so. Then, just as unconsciously, you could spit that energy onto someone else. You could feel unhappy for no reason other than you picked up another person's energy and are trying to get rid of it. You can see how this can become a dangerous energetic cycle.

When your psychic boundaries are intact your energy, your aura, is kept comfortably close to you. You do not want your aura to get too big and wide open, unless your aura is full of your own energy (which will happen as you do your spiritual work). Spiritual masters have huge auras. If you are not yet a spiritual master, bring all your energy in close to you and place a protective ring of light around you. Ground yourself frequently during the day to help you create and maintain healthy psychic boundaries.

Cords

Cords are energetic attachments. An energetic cord can come from someone with you, from someone nearby, or from someone on the other side of the world. Energetic cords know no physical limits. An energetic cord allows another person to connect with your energy, opening you to be energetically depleted, which feels like you are being attacked by an energy vampire.

If a person is intentionally cording with you, you will feel it, you will know. Sometimes an energetic cord is created unconsciously You may feel profoundly tired after a conversation on the phone with a friend or family member. A cord was probably attached. Immediately say, "I release all cords."

You may be surprised who will connect with you, seemingly out of the blue. That person has an energetic attachment to you. That person may not be malicious and they may not have corded with you on purpose. That they have corded with you does not mean that you should delete them permanently from your life. People will make cords. You make cords and you may not even know you are doing so. It is a good thing to clear cords for both your own benefit and the benefit of whomever you are connected to by a cord.

To Release Cords

Close your eyes and imagine your auric field, the energetic space that surrounds your body. Say, "I release all cords and attachments that are connected to my auric field." Archangel Michael is an excellent archangel to call on for releasing cords. If you choose to call on Archangel Michael say, "Archangel Michael, release all cords and attachments that are connected to my auric field."

Releasing cords is preferable to cutting cords. Cutting cords can be intense and extreme, potentially causing pain to the other person. You never want to cause harm to another person, especially if that person was not even aware they were creating an energetic cord with you. Say, "I release energetic cords with (the person's name). I ask that healing light be sent to the owner of this cord so she may receive the healing she needs." This allows that person to have the right connection with their higher power. When a person is attached to his higher power, he will not need to attach to you.

As you continue to work with your energy field, you will notice less and less cording because others will not be able to attach to you and you will be aware when you are cording with someone else. As you work with the protective healing light, you will experience these types of attachments less and less.

Energetic Protection

You can protect yourself energetically and prevent inappropriate cording, attachments, and interference.

The Violet Flame

The violet flame is an energy of protection and transmutation that is connected to the energetic protection of the Ascended Master, St. Germain and the Archangel Michael. Visualize a violet flame around you when you want psychic protection.

Light

Bring in three rings of three-dimensional light and set the intention that it will accompany you everywhere. See the light surrounding your auric field, 360 degrees around you. See rings of golden, pink, green, violet, or purple light. Any of these colors will work. These are healing and protective colors, but if you resonate with other colors, use them.

You can also bring down a column of pure white light. Visualize a column of light and see it completely enveloping you.

Psychic Boundaries with Family

When you have family members who are also intuitive, you may feel that you never get a break from them because they are in your psychic awareness. They may psychically push their energy on you, and you may be inadvertently directing psychic energy at them. You want to stay connected to your family but you don't want them inappropriately in your psychic space. Practice saying, "I bring all my attention and awareness and all of my energy back to myself. I ask that all energy I have given away or left behind return to me now." Bring your conscious energy and awareness close into you to complete the practice.

When you know you will be seeing a family member or speaking with them on the phone, practice saying, "I am putting up a shield. I am putting up a shield for (family member title) whom I love, because I need to maintain healthy psychic boundaries." That is okay and completely functional to do.

Sometimes your family member is part of a dream sequence. Dream sequences and psychic information you receive before an event happens can affect the outcome of that event.

When John was a little boy he had a dream that his sister, with whom he was very strongly psychically connected, hit him over the head with a brush. The next day he was standing in front of the mirror, his sister standing behind him. He had an intuitive flash of the dream and dodged out of the way just as she was trying to hit him on the head with the brush! Clearly there are real-life physical benefits to following your intuition. Following your intuition could save you from a bump on the head, or worse.

Head-jumping

Projecting your psychic energy into someone else's head space, head-jumping, is a strict no-no. Many psychics head-jump into other people's head space, not to maliciously hurt the other person, but because they have inappropriate psychic boundaries. When you jump into someone else's head space you are misplacing your power. If you place your power and energy inside another person with the intention of "fixing" them, you are assuming that you know what is best for them - and you never know what is best for another person. Only Source energy knows what is best for them - not you, not your teacher, not your teacher's teacher. Only Source energy knows what's best.

Don't ever jump in to someone else's energy field and offer healing. As you become healed and learn to ground yourself, you can then ground other people. You can ask your angels and guides to send healing energy, but you cannot place healing energy around another person, nor can you jump into their energy field and try to mess around in there, unless you have been given permission by that person to do so.

If you ever experience an instant headache that goes away after a little bit, someone is probably in your head space. Another person has unconsciously or consciously connected an energy beam to your sixth chakra. When you feel this, call on Archangel Michael and say, "Archangel Michael, release this energy now. Send this energy back to its owner with a warning to stay out of other people's lives and experience and focus on their own life."

As you are learning to create appropriate psychic boundaries, remember to bring your energy in, close to you, releasing attachments to cords, making sure your consciousness is not rubbing up in anyone else's consciousness, making sure you are not head-jumping. If you have a very intense sixth chakra, or if you are an indigo child, or if you have a strong awareness of your sixth chakra, place your awareness in the back of your head. With an overactive sixth chakra, your tendency is to probe with it, seeking out information. In order for you to respect other peoples' psychic boundaries, perceive others from the back part of your mind. This will keep your energy from invading another person's psychic field.

Energy Too Close In

Just as you don't want to be right on top of a person when you talk to them, you don't want to be too close to another person with your own energy. You don't want to spread your energy around or beam your energy inappropriately at another person. Many a healer has said, "I am just going to beam my heart energy and it is going to heal the world." The concept is good, but even this kind of intention can become perpetrator energy,

energy that is used without the permission of those you wish to receive it. Even if it is heart energy, if you are assuming others want to receive it, assuming you know what is best for others, which you do not, is a form of energy perpetration. Perhaps the person you are inappropriately beaming your heart energy towards needs to feel angry or sad or depressed. You do not know what process is best for another person, so unless your energy is being asked for, keep it close to yourself.

As an energetic, aware, intuitive individual, you need to know that you can shine your light from within and without, without directing it or blurring the edges of your aura. If you push your energy too far out, you could be pushing into other people's space. Know the parameters of your energy field. Keep your energy close in. If you are full of radiant energy, it is fine to emanate that energy out into the world, just don't direct that energy to a specific person or persons without their consent.

If you are extremely sensitive, it can be very trying to experience life fending off other people's energy. Remember to place the violet flame of protection around you. You can also place a circle of golden, green, or pink healing light around you. Direct that light into yourself so it becomes a protective healing light around you. The light is not a barrier, as you do not want to form a barricade around you, but you do want an appropriate filter.

Spiritual Healing:
Filling up after Energy Clearing

As you ground, whether you are connecting with Earth and creating a grounding cord, placing your energy in your will center, asking universal healing energy to heal the sore spots, or tapping just below your collar bone and connecting your selves to each other, you are creating a base, a center, from which you will rid yourself of all energy that is not of your highest good. Rid yourself of any energy that is not of your highest good by dropping it down to the center of Earth, sending it out into space, or simply releasing it from you.

After the energy clears, you will have little cavities or caverns inside your energy field that are now open, free of the debris that was clogging that space. Blocks removed leave energetic openings. Spiritual healing places light into the spaces where energy has been released from your body.

Bring in golden-white light, light that looks like honey. Imagine your body as an outline or feel the light in your body. Imagine spiritual, healing light covering your body and see that light coming down from above, or up from below. See the healing light filtering into and filling the little caverns.

As you see the light filling the caverns, continue to feel the spiritual healing. Let it flow all the way up into your head, through your hands, into your body. Continue to fill the caverns, allowing the light to energetically release out into your aura just a little bit, ensuring that there are no holes or parts that still need to be filled. See this light patching, or filling in, any energy that seems flat, dull, or gray, or any places where you might feel you need energy in your body. See the energy going to those places. When you do this, you will feel a significant difference in your energy field.

It is vital to do this spiritual healing because wherever you have cleared attachments or inappropriate energetic connections, you have left holes and spaces in your aura that are wide open for energy you may not want to enter.

Always do your spiritual healing after you have released cords. As soon as you release cords, bring in the golden light to fill in where the released cords have left a place that needs healing. Clean your aura and your energetic bodies as you clean your physical body - with care and attention to all that needs maintenance and more detailed attention.

When Someone Makes You Their Savior

Sometimes when a person is in crisis and you are the one who helps her, she can easily put you into the role of savior. Therapists and healers often experience this transference. When someone thinks of you as being their savior, coming to you first and not to their own higher power, that person will attach an energetic cord to you. This can be tricky because as a healer, you probably have at least some desire to be needed or wanted. You need to check in with yourself and make sure you are not seeing yourself as the source of healing, but as the vehicle for the healing power of Source energy.

When a client feels that you are their only hope, their savior, and has attached one or more energetic cords to you, you need to release those cords. Before you work with that person, you need to do energetic light shielding. Place the violet or gold flame around them and around yourself. Direct a channel of light from above over the client. This way they cannot receive the energy from you, but will receive it from Source. You may have to step back a little bit energetically as you place protection around them, giving them what they truly need - their own connection to Source energy.

If you are in a line of work where your clients are in trauma and crisis on a daily basis, you may often be considered the savior. You need to do energetic light shielding at the beginning and at the end of your daily work with clients. Before you sit with the first client, place the violet flame of protection around your body. This can prevent some energetic cords from forming. If the cords get formed anyway (it happens), some of them will be burned away by the violet flame. For the cords that are not dealt with by the violet flame, call on Archangel Michael. Say, "Archangel Michael, I ask you to release all cords from me now and return them, with grace and love, to all others." Do this every night before bed.

Manage Your Aura

Another technique to help you create appropriate boundaries is to manage the level of your aura. Ask yourself where your aura is on a scale from 1 to 10 or 1 to 100. Is it at full blast or at zero? Is the pilot light being blown out or are you a raging fire, wasting energy? Feel where the middle ground is and strive to maintain that. If you are feeling low in energy or vulnerable, stoke up your energy. If your aura is too big, too intrusive, pull it back in.

You need to be aware of how wide open, out of focus, or blurry your aura might be. Check in often to see how appropriate the boundaries around your aura are. Ask yourself if your aura is in focus, if it is pulled in close to you, and if your boundaries are intact. Practice being aware and conscious of your boundaries.

Be aware of which part of your aura your consciousness is occupying. It is best to place your consciousness in the middle of your aura. If you are way back in your aura, you will create a huge energy field in front of you. You can bombard people with your energy when you do this. You will know you are doing this because people will automatically act defensively around you, trying to keep your energy off of them. The farther back you are in your aura, the more your back becomes vulnerable to energy coming in that is not yours. The back, where the aura is thin, will be more permeable.

If you stand at the very front edge of your aura, you have lots of energy behind you. That can feel scary to people because they feel you have something behind you, but they do not know what it is. This creates the same energy as a close talker, with the sixth chakra inappropriately beaming forward, jumping into other people's privacy. Remember that this type of head-jumping is a strict no-no.

Instead of being in the back or front of your aura, be in the middle of it. Ask yourself where in your aura you are focusing. Trust your intuitive voice to give you that information. Adjust accordingly to get back to the middle of your aura if you are not there. It is your place of power.

Working with Your Empathic Abilities

If you have empathic abilities, you can actually feel the pain that another person is experiencing. You feel their pain as real pain in your body.

Let's say someone's leg hurts and you begin to feel pain in your leg. It feels like you are taking on that person's energy. This could mean you have healed them because you have taken energy from them. They may then experience less pain because you have taken it on. Sometimes it just means that you took on the energetic blueprint. They are still in pain, and now, so are you.

You have to make sure that you are not matching their energy, that you are having appropriate psychic boundaries, that you are not blending or merging energy with them. Bring your energy close into your energy field. Ground yourself. Release the energy you have picked up. If the energy (pain) is in a specific body part, you will actually see or feel or know that body part up close, or however you experience your psychic abilities. You might be able to see the energy in the body part where it is lodged. However you see it is how it is.

Drain all the energy out that is not yours, all the energy that is not for your highest good. Bring that energy down into the core of the earth where it can be healed, transmuted into positive energy. Then bring in extra healing energy for yourself.

Let's say you know a person has an injury or he is just not feeling so great. You pick this up intuitively. Immediately ground yourself and ground the other person. Then place a healing energy around the area in their body where they have an injury or where you feel the issue lies. Do this to protect yourself. Do it immediately. As you learn to automatically ground and protect yourself, you will notice that you will not pick up other people's energies. That is a good thing!

Receiving Unwanted Information

As you are opening up and developing your psychic abilities you are going to see and feel things that you may not want to see and feel, things you have not asked for. The more you develop your psychic skills, the less this will happen. In order to deflect unwanted and unasked for information from coming in, you need to ground often, placing the violet or gold flame of protection around you.

Also call on your guides and angels. Tell them you need a psychic helmet. Put on that psychic helmet when you are out in public so as not to attract random information from other people. Take off the psychic helmet when you want to receive information. See the helmet as a hat or a crown, but see it as something that is completely covering your crown and forehead.

The more you work with your guidance, continuing to ground, release, and protect, the less you will receive unwanted information. As your personal discernment develops you will know what is for your highest good and what is not. If unwanted information does penetrate into your awareness, clear it out, like tossing unwanted mail.

You can also ask if this information is good and necessary for you. Ask your body, ask your knowingness, ask your guides. You do not have to figure out everything on your own. Ask for help and guidance from your own guides and angels, from your Higher Self.

Monitoring Your Own Psychic Energy

Observe your own energy as you go through your day. When you first meet someone, notice your own energy. Are you reticent and reserved, weary? Are you putting up huge psychic shields that are inappropriate to the situation? Are you projecting your energy strongly into the world, at other people? It is excellent practice to notice your own energy and monitor its flow and receptivity. Here are a few monitoring processes you can do to remain aware of your energy and keep it in check.

Rose Visualization

Visualize roses all around you. Plant roses around yourself and see rose buds coming up all around you. Roses are beautiful and fragrant. They don't push anyone away but they do have thorns. The thorns will prevent entry into your psychic space if anyone tries to come into it inappropriately. Aim for a middle ground of welcoming and healthy distance until you can decide how close to let a person get into your psychic space.

Monitor Your Energy

Do not shove your own energy out into the world. You do not want to head-jump into another person's psychic space. You also don't want to blare your energy as if it were coming through a megaphone. Watch your own energy level, especially with new people and in new situations. This will increase your self-awareness and give you information about how to monitor yourself appropriately in any situation.

Chapter 6

Analytical Mind / Intuitive Mind

Both your analytical mind and your intuitive mind have value to you as you navigate through your life. In Western cultures we are taught to value the analytical mind over the intuitive mind, so the analytical mind receives more attention and more training. Like training and building muscles, the ones you focus your attention on and the ones you focus on developing, will develop. So it is with your mind. Our culture has taught you to focus and grow your analytical mind, so it is highly developed.

To train and develop your intuitive mind, your intuitive instinct, you need to make a shift in your value system. You need to see the inherent value in developing your intuition so you will focus your attention on learning the skills of developing and growing your intuitive muscles. Changing your value system is an internal process. The ego, which represents your analytical mind, needs to be managed appropriately for your mind to work in balance between the analytical and the intuitive.

The analytical mind works differently from the intuitive mind. Each part of your mind is best used in the areas it was designed to affect. For instance, let's say you are at the grocery store to purchase organic butter. There are many brands of butter to choose from. How do you make the decision and end up with the butter that is ideal for you?

You read the information on the package and analyze the information for facts about the butter. The analytical mind helps you discern the brand to choose.

The intuitive mind is tackling a different issue: Is butter good for your body right now? When you look at the packages of butter you will have a certain feeling in your body, or you might see an image in your mind, or you might hear something. You might know that butter is what your body does, or does not, need that day. Your intuitive mind can give you that information.

Ideally, you want the analytical mind to work in partnership with the intuitive mind. Each part of the mind has gifts and abilities. To function in their highest potential, the intuitive and analytical parts of the mind must each be clean and clear, working in tandem, each part focused on what is appropriate in any particular situation.

A client of ours was driving on the highway when she had an impulsive, fleeting thought come through her mind that told her to get off the highway at the exit coming up quickly on her right. That exit was miles from the exit she usually took, but the instruction came through so strongly and clearly she veered off and took the exit. We know it was her intuitive mind because the direction came quickly, firmly, and was specifically directive, but did not seem to have any logical reasoning. It turns out that, just moments later, there was a nine-car pileup on the highway that she would have been a part of had she not turned off. Her higher guidance was directing her, through her intuition, saving herself a lot of grief because she followed the guidance.

The ego requires concrete proof, so it needs to hear stories of how the intuitive mind saves and protects you. That is how the ego learns to trust the intuition. It is important to remind the ego of times when your intuition saved the day.

Some years ago, moments before a New York City blackout, John was on the subway. Something told him to get off the train right away, even though he was many stops away from his usual one. He questioned himself, wondering if he should go or stay. The train stopped and he bolted off, just as the doors were closing. The blackout hit as he was walking through the underground station. The people stuck on that train were in the dark for hours and had to crawl out through the tunnel system. What a save that was!

You can encourage the ego with stories like these. The ego can then see that your intuitive instinct can be trusted and can be critically helpful.

Sometimes random or fleeting thoughts come in as you are busy doing other things. Fleeting thoughts are usually your intuition. They are often direct, knowing, and are positive in nature. Random thoughts that feel scattered and erratic are usually negative in nature, like thoughts that make you feel fearful. Intuitive thoughts are similar to fleeting thoughts. They seem to come forward in a certain part of your head, as if you can actually feel them in a certain area in your mind.

Test your thoughts. As you go through your day, play with your thoughts to see if what appear to be random thoughts are true or not. Perhaps you randomly think of a person. You don't know why you are thinking about that person. Later that day, maybe you see them or hear something about them. Random thoughts that feel solid and direct often are intuitive flashes.

Intuition is not linear. You need to test your intuition so you become familiar with how to recognize it. Because your intuitive instinct is unique to you, the only way you can really know your intuition is to play with it, testing different thoughts and feelings. You might think you are making things up. Many people feel that when they are first learning to work with their intuition.

Do not affirm any negative treatment of your intuitive thought. Affirm only the positive treatment of your intuition. When you tell yourself that you are making things up practice saying, "I am correct most of the time, even if I don't know that I am correct." Affirm your intuition and it will grow.

Sometimes your analytical mind will butt in as you are trying to test your intuitive mind. You will be checking in with your intuition, receiving information, and then another voice, your ego, will pipe in. You can't stop your ego from giving its opinion. That is its nature. After you have proven that follow-ing your intuition is for your highest good, your ego will calm down.

John and I were camping at the perfect campsite because not only was it breathtakingly beautiful, pristine, and quiet but it was also near a flush toilet facility. At the break of dawn I was en route to the facility and decided to get my toothbrush out of the car. We had rented a jeep-type vehicle that had a remote locking device on a key chain. I unlocked the car and rum-maged about for my toothbrush. Truth be told, no matter how well I think I have organized the car for a road trip, whatever I am looking for, I have the hardest time finding it. That morning was no different.

As I was rummaging about the car I had an intuitive flash that I would lock the keys in the car. The thought and the action happened instantaneously, but had that super slowed down, slow-motion feeling. I thought the thought and heard the car door close, seemingly all in the same moment. When I heard the click of the car door and saw the keys on the front driver's seat, I had that sinking feeling that I had just created what could turn into a major hassle.

John jumped up out of the tent and said, "Did you just lock the keys in the car?" I replied, "I did but I can't think about that right now. I have to go to the bathroom." I headed off to the bathroom and immediately did what any New Yorker would do: think about who I could call to help open the door. It never crossed my mind for even a moment that I would be able to open that car myself. I came to the conclusion that I would walk to the campground store in a few hours when they would be open and call AAA road service. I figured this would be an all-day affair and we would just enjoy the park until the fix-it guys appeared. We had food aplenty and views and hiking trails and oh well, it could be worse!

John had a different idea.

As I returned to the campsite I saw him standing by the car with a washcloth wedged into the tiny crack between the door and the car body. It seemed the car door was not quite slammed all the way shut. I went into the tent, crawled into my sleeping bag, covered my head with a pillow, and pleaded with my angels to help us get into the car. Rationally, I didn't think there was any way John could get into that car. But I knew John had abilities way beyond the limits of my own imagination and my belief in angelic intervention allowed me to just turn it over to them. I let myself relax into the knowing that whatever happened, all was well. It was just another camping adventure.

In about five minutes I heard the car door click open. I jumped out of the tent and saw John standing by the open car door, tent stake in his hand and the biggest, triumphant smile on his face.

"You opened the car!" I exclaimed. "How did you do it?"

John doesn't drive, has never owned a car, and did not have AAA emergency road service as an option. He told me he had been determined to get the door open. He just knew he was going to get into that car.

He first wedged the washcloth into the crack to see if that would nudge the door open. That didn't work. Then he picked up a stick and tried to slide it down in the tiny space between the door and the car. He got the stick in there but couldn't see how to get the stick turned around to hit the lock on the door.

He started to feel frustrated and angry that he couldn't figure out what to do. As he felt the frustration he consciously bid it aside and got supremely quiet inside his mind. He asked his guides and angels to show him what to do. He released judgment and frustration and just listened for direction.

Higher guidance told him to take a pole from the tent because it was thin and flexible. He was able to get the pole into the car and then he heard, "The keys are on the front seat." The keys were on the seat, face down. Then he heard, "Flip them over." He caught the ring of the keys in the tent pole and flipped the keys over so the button side was up. The "open" button was right next to the "alarm" button. Ever so gently but firmly, with clearest intention, he pushed the pole to hit the open button. And voila! The door clicked open.

We were jubilant. Not only because he got the door open and not only because he hit the open button instead of the deafening car alarm button (which would have caused quite the stir in the sleepy campsite). We were jubilant because he had quieted his mind enough to hear his guidance and because he followed it!

Within an hour we were enjoying a lovely breakfast outside Durango, marveling at the power of connecting to and following guidance, combining the analytical mind and the intuitive mind to get us out of a challenging situation.

Egoic Voice vs. Intuitive Voice

Let's say you are at a crossroads and you are trying to decide whether to go right or left. A soft voice, which is usually your intuition, says, "Go right."

Another voice, loudly and perhaps even abrasively says, "Go left!" or "Which way? Left or right?" The egoic voice is often erratic, bossy, freaked out, scared, and trying to control the situation. The voice of the ego is bossy and has a controlling form of expression or tone. The intuitive voice is soft and has a quiet, gentle presence. The intuitive voice can be heard between conscious thoughts.

Talk to your ego to calm and soothe it. Say, "Ego, I need you to be quiet now so I can listen to my intuition." Eventually your ego will calm down. Then ask, "Intuition, which way should I go, left or right?" Continue to ask and practice discerning between the different energies of your thoughts. This will help you tap into your inner voice, your intuitive voice.

The development of the intuitive voice tends to run through the family lineage. Like veins of crystals running through the Earth, there are lineage lines that carry intuitive gifts. The intuitive gift can come through in different ways through the generations. Your grandmother could be a psychic detective, but you may not be. You might be a psychic healer, physically or energetically. Your soul energy will carry the imprint of the intuitive. How it manifests in your life will be unique to you. You have to investigate and find your own unique gift.

Sometimes intuitive information comes through mixed up or backwards. This is intuitive dyslexia. Images come through with flipped emotions or the energy is the opposite of what it really is. This is an issue of fine-tuning. As you receive healings yourself, keeping yourself tuned up, the pathways get cleared and the information can come through more clearly. Wires do get crossed and blocks can occur that cause disconnections and distortions. It can also be the ego trying to confuse you in order to maintain control.

Play with asking to be shown information in the correct order and the correct orientation. Continue to ask questions. As one thing clarifies, ask another, and then another. Grill and test your intuition to strengthen it. When you feel you have played enough, give yourself a rest and relax. The relaxation time will help you integrate what you are learning.

Often, information will come through dreams or through symbols in your waking life. If you see visual symbols in your waking life, you are probably clairvoyant. The messages we receive in dreams can be psychic information or they could also be ways you are processing information. The whole topic of dreams is a book unto itself!

The more you develop and grow your intuitive skills, the more you will experience consequences for not following your intuitive guidance. Symptoms and experiences will magnify because your awareness is growing. Your intuition is looking out for your best interests all the time. As you learn to pay attention to your intuition and learn to trust and follow its guidance, you can be protected from many mishaps.

Intuitive Manifestation

While you are in a meditative state, in focused attention, or in deep concentration, you can connect more deeply to Source energy and draw to you what you want. You can do this in several ways.

Be impeccably clear in your intentions. Be in a happy state of mind and concentrate on what you are thinking. Think happy, relaxed thoughts.

Think of your sixth chakra, your third eye area, connecting with your crown (seventh chakra), creating a beam of light that spreads energy out into the universe. Place into that light an image or a short saying of what you would like to bring into your life. Then feel the feeling that what you desire is already with you. The longer you can connect to the image/thought without being distracted, the more energy or life force you are sending into the universe to create what you want in your life.

Another way of doing intuitive manifestation is to place your mind at your second chakra, the will center, a few inches below your belly button. See your second chakra grow bigger and brighter, gathering energy, becoming a magnet for what you want in your life, what you desire. See pictures and images of what you desire coming towards you.

There is also a connection to your intuition that is impossible to articulate and cannot be understood by the conscious mind. That connection, or understanding, is a place in your mind where you do not hold any judgment. In that place you feel connected to everything but not in a verbal way, not in a way where things are given titles or definitions. This place is expansive, wordless, a void. The void is where creation begins, and where intuitive manifestation begins. In order to manifest, you need to connect to the universal void, where all creation begins.

Try to shut down some of your mental ideas about what intuition is. Allow yourself to feel connected to everything and nothing - the nameless, wordless energy. When you do this you are able to connect more deeply with your intuitive abilities. If you are clairvoyant you will be able to receive much more accurate and clear pictures. A door can open to more information, relieving the linear mind from the trap of mind control. The controlled mind wants to label and categorize everything. But that is only one, limited perspective, not an expansive, universal perspective.

The intuitive plane of awareness is different than the conscious, controlling mind. To access the intuitive plane, begin by letting your eyes relax. Scan over what is going on rather than trying to pinpoint, label, and title every single thing. As soon as you title and label a thing, you slightly alter that thing from its original expression of itself. The ego loves to title and label, as that makes the ego feel safe. Reign in your ego so you can believe what you are seeing and what you are experiencing as valid. This will help you step into the wordless, unspoken, vast energy that exists in the universe. This is an excellent exercise to help you relieve stress and anxiety, to spring into the place where anxiety and stress do not exist. When you are relieved of stress and anxiety you are more able to access the intelligence of your intuitive instinct.

The intuitive mind is nonlinear, like an amoeba. Your intuition will answer any question you ask it. You have to move the ego out of the way in order to accurately hear your intuition. Ground yourself. Clear your mind. See your mind as a blank slate where the intuition can place the answers to your questions and direct you safely through your life. Use your analytical mind for puzzle solving and practical discernment. Use your intuitive mind to guide you. Using both your intuitive mind and your analytical mind to help you navigate through your life will make your journey more enjoyable, directing you safely home.

Chapter 7

Your Intuitive Style

As you experiment and play with the experience of connecting to your Higher Self, your higher knowing, you will come to understand that intuition styles differ and each person has their own unique understanding of their intuition. As you begin to grow and develop, learning to trust your intuitive instinct, you will see it grow and unfold for you. Each person has a particular intuitive style. You may find yourself using a combination of styles.

To develop your intuitive style, you need to be open to doing so. Practice saying, "I am open to my instinct and to finding my intuitive style. I am going to play like a child with my intuition. I am open to being instinctual and to finding my intuitive style, playing with wonder and amazement. It is going to be such fun!" And then see what unfolds. Notice what starts happening in your awareness and in your life. Keep track of what is, and is not, working for you.

Play little intuitive games with yourself to help you identify your intuitive style. Try to guess the color of the next car coming down the street. Or try to guess the amount of your purchases at the grocery store. Or try to guess the color of the hair of the next person you will see. Playing these little games will help you begin to see how many times you are correct. If you are not correct, do not condemn yourself. Continue to affirm when you are correct. Affirming your intuitive instinct will build your intuitive confidence.

As you begin to connect with your intuitive style, play with it. Allow yourself to be any or all of the psychic styles. Don't categorize yourself rigidly as you could begin to receive information in many ways. Ask your guidance and your higher self to help you know your instinctive capabilities. The more you feed and nourish your instinctual self, the more your intuition will grow and evolve. Psychic styles are categorized as: clairvoyant, clairsentient, clairaudient, claircognizant, and clairolfactory.

Clairvoyance is the ability to see and is focused in the eyes. If you are clairvoyant, you will see something outside in the everyday world just like you see a concrete item in your hand, or you may close your eyes and see pictures or visions like movies in your mind.

Clairsentience is feeling. As a clairsentient, you feel energy inside of your body. You get a feeling in your gut, or you may feel something actually move inside of you. The feeling in your gut is not like a stomachache. It feels more like energy coursing through you or energy that you become aware of in your physical body. The feeling usually comes with a knowing, a sense about what the feeling of the energy is describing to you. You can also feel someone else's energy - their emotional state, their feeling state. Clairsentients are often healers. Clairsentience borders on being empathic. As an empath, you would probably feel, in your own body, the issues someone else is having in their body. Empaths tend to take on physical pain of others, clairsentients don't.

There are subtle differences between being an empath and being clairsentient. As a clairsentient, you feel the deepest parts of another person, things that that person may not be aware of. As an empath, you would tend to feel what another person is feeling. You can feel their body and their ailments in your own body. Clairsentients have more psychic and healing abilities than empaths. A clairsentient can literally feel the deepest energy inside of another person and intuitively know how to heal that person. An empath feels the symptoms but may not be able to go to the core of where they originated, as a clairsentient does. Healing happens on the core level, not on the level of the manifested symptom.

For instance, a person can have chronic fatigue. As an empath, you would feel the exhaustion and the depression of that person. As a clairsentient, you would feel these same things, but you would also feel and know the core reasons the chronic fatigue is manifesting. You would go to the core to release blocks that facilitates healing.

Clairaudients hear. Information is received through hearing. Clairaudients often hear very specific information and spiritual music.

Claircognizance is a knowing. You don't know why you know, you just do.

Clairolfactory is the intuitive ability that is experienced through your sense of smell. The sense of smell, and what the smells translate to in your awareness, provides guidance. Sometimes a place will have a scent that connects with your awareness. Sometimes a person will give off scents that trigger something in you - a memory or a knowing. During healings people can often give off a foul smell as toxins are being released.

I am claircognizant and usually just know what I know when I know it. Sometimes I am clairaudient. I hear words that feel like gentle nudges. That's how I found the stash of rose hips.

I was foraging around my yard for branches and such to make a large arrangement for one of our group gatherings. It was December, before the Solstice of the Golden Dawn, and the pickings were slim. I had some lovely evergreen fir branches, but what I really wanted was branches with berries. I drove around town looking for some trees that needed a few berried branches trimmed. I couldn't find any along the roadsides where I usually collect materials.

I ended up going to the Good Will store to look for some glass bowls for the ritual we were planning for the solstice gathering, and as I got back into my car to head out for more berry foraging, I heard a soft voice in my head say, "Drive behind the

Good Will building." I didn't even know there was a "behind" part to the Good Will building, and I certainly had never been there. I drove around to the back, and to my delight, there was a very large bed of wild rose bushes! The stems were two to three feet long, covered with bright red berries, and relatively thornfree. What a find!

I began to trim away at the bushes and collected a magnificent bouquet of brilliant orangey-red rose hips, perfect for my arrangement. It was truly a win-win situation. Many people enjoyed the rose hips that evening, and the plant would benefit from the pruning.

My higher guidance knew where those rose hips were and, because I listened, I found them.

Each intuitive has a variation and often a combination of psychic styles. As you name the different psychic styles, it becomes easier to recognize them in your own experience. And as intuition shows up in your body or in your mind, it is good and important to affirm it because when you affirm your intuition, you develop it. Experiment with and test your abilities.

Techniques for Testing
Your Intuitive Style

Take a few minutes and try this exercise. Whatever information you receive is correct. There is no wrong answer.

Say, "I am opening my awareness to my highest intuitive gift. I am going to let my intuition tell me what my highest gift is. This may be through a physical feeling in my body, seeing an image in my head, hearing a melody in my mind or out loud, or having a deep knowing within my mind."

Did you receive an answer?

Whatever answer you receive is correct for you.

Are You Clairvoyant?

In this technique you will create and connect to a viewing screen in the back of your head. Take a few deep breaths. Imagine yourself in a room - your intuitive place in your mind. See yourself in a very comfortable position, perhaps on a chaise lounge, in the back of a movie theater that has a big, blank screen. Maybe you're eating some popcorn, or some other favorite food. Maybe you can smell your favorite smell.

As you see the big, blank, white movie screen, ask yourself, "Is it in my highest interest to develop my intuition?" As you ask yourself this question, visualize a rose, a pencil-drawn outline of a rose. Once you have an image of the rose, analyze it. See this outline of a rose begin to grow. What color is it? Is the rose part of a bush that is rooted into the ground? What do the leaves look like? How many different flowers are there on the plant? Is there one type of rose or a couple of different roses?

When something is good for you, the rose will appear brightly colored, vibrant, lush and healthy. The rose will be rooted to the ground or appear to be floating in outer space. When things do not feel good for you, the rose will be funky. Maybe it is off to the side a little bit, or droopy. Maybe it is overgrown and a little scary.

Analyze your rose and you will begin to see a pattern. Let go of your conscious thoughts and allow your intuition to read the rose. You can ask any question at all, but a question that has a yes or no answer is best and easiest to read. If the situation is complicated, break the questions down to a series of yes/no questions.

Practicing creating a viewing screen is an excellent way to begin to connect to your intuition. You have to be patient with yourself because your body can only handle so much at one time. You have to stay realistic. Maybe you can only do this for five minutes at a time. That is fine. Five minutes is better than nothing. Five minutes will turn into ten minutes, which will turn into fifteen minutes, and then twenty, and then pretty soon you will be spending more and more time in the meditative state. You will have to set an alarm for yourself because you will not be able to come back from the ethers or from your intuitive room and from connecting with your guidance.

Are You Clairsentient?

Now let's practice feeling in the body. Feel your heart. How does it feel? What are the sensations coming from your heart right now? Connect with those you love through your heart chakra. Pick any loved one in your life and connect with them heart-to-heart. Feel that person's experience through your heart.

Now feel your own second chakra, a few inches below your belly button. How does that feel? Feel the emotions that are there. What are those emotions? Now try to feel the emotions of the person, the loved one, you chose to feel. Try to feel their emotions. How does that feel? If you tapped into the feeling right away and could feel the pull of energy in your 2nd chakra, you are probably clairsentient and/or have empathic capabilities

If you did not connect in your body, that is totally fine. As with all these exercises, exactly how you are is exactly how you are supposed to be! There is no right or wrong. Each of us connects to our intuition in our own unique way.

Are You Clairaudient?

Focus your attention on Archangel Michael. If you hear beautiful music arising around him, music that has an energy and a vibration when he or other angelic beings are near, you are probably clairaudient. You may hear music or actual words spoken as guidance. You may hear the music and/or words inside your head or outside your head.

Colors also emit a sound vibration, a resonance that some can hear. Focus on the color indigo. Now listen for golden-white light. Now focus on deep, vital red. If you could hear any of these colors, you probably have clairaudient abilities.

Are You Claircognizant?

If you are claircognizant answers come quickly as thought forms into your consciousness. If you think you might be claircognizant think of a question you want answered. Sit quietly. Ask the question. If a clear thought form, often quieter with less of an energetic charge than your usual thoughts, comes into your mind, test that thought form to see if it is correct - if it is, you probably have claircognizant abilities.

Are You Clairolfactory?

The olfactory sense, your sense of smell, is the most primal of all the senses. Smells can trigger all kinds of memories and emotional responses. Most people naturally use their sense of smell to determine if something will be to their liking or not. The more you train and develop your sense of smell, the more effective it can serve you as an accurate barometer of a wide range of experiences.

Do you ever enter a room and notice a smell that triggers a familiarity or knowingness in you? Do you notice a smell coming off a person and you then have a knowing about that person? That would be the olfactory intuitive sense working its magic.

Your personal intuitive style, whatever it may be, is perfect and right for you. As you practice using your instinct, your own intuitive style will become obvious to you. And as you understand more about your intuitive style, it will evolve and become more complex. You might find yourself becoming adept in several intuitive, instinctual styles.

Chapter 8

Healing

Healing is a process of clearing and releasing patterns of disharmony and trauma. Clearing the path for energy to flow within the systems of the body brings the body into full harmony and balance, the state of unconditional love for self and for others.

Western culture tends to be symptom-oriented. The symptom is treated but the core root of the dysfunction and disease is often overlooked, especially if the core issues are emotional or related to karmic patterns of trauma. If only the symptoms are treated, the problems will persist. Healing is a process of treating the core issues, addressing the mental, physical, emotional, and spiritual root causes of disease and dysfunction.

Every moment you are responding to your experiences, processing external stimuli coming into your energy field. You are either embracing what comes towards you or repelling what feels scary and harmful. Accumulation of the fight or flight responses to information and stimuli causes traumatic blocks within the energy field. No matter how big or how small, this process is ongoing. Depending on the level of trauma, the blocks will be larger or smaller.

Habitual emotional patterns like grief, loss, abandonment, and sadness turn into behaviors that create stuck energy. This stuck energy becomes like locks in the body, locks that prohibit life force energy to move into all parts of the body. The locked-out areas are depleted of life force, creating atrophy and disease.

When You Are Emotionally Triggered

You can have an emotional response to an event or another person, a patterned response, repeating an early childhood or past life experience. This is called a trigger. The most important thing about triggers is to be aware of them. You may be unaware that you are being triggered. You may have to get triggered many times before you realize that you are being triggered.

Identifying your own triggers is the first step in the healing process. Acknowledging that the trigger exists helps you see that the trigger is creating an emotional response, a block. The trigger alerts you that there is energy trapped or pooled above a specific chakra. This blockage needs to be cleared and released or disease can set in. The trigger is a gift to you from your higher self. The trigger directs you to where healing is required.

The emotional, physical, and etheric bodies are all connected. When you do physical healing energy work, you are also healing the emotional and physical bodies. Work with your psychological responses as well as your energetic levels to bring up triggers and release trapped, unexpressed emotions. Energetic healing dissipates energy, decreasing emotional responses. As you work on your energetic body, you will come to understand that the energy and psychic debris you have taken on is not necessarily yours. You do not have to claim or hold on to any energy that is not yours. In truth, that energy needs to be sent out in the universe to be recycled. Your job is to tend to and care for your energetic body the same way you care for your physical body.

You need mental health days and vacation from your busyness in order to clear out psychic debris. As you work on all levels, you will come to realize that all the bodies are connected and that you are able to eliminate triggered responses from your experience. Trigger response time will be shorter or the triggers could be permanently removed.

Sometimes an emotional response will lead you to insights about yourself, like delusions of needing to be perfect or needing to be some way other than you are. Emotional responses are conditions you have decided to carry, but doing so was not necessarily a conscious choice. Often these patterns are coping mechanisms that were put in place to manage difficult situations and persons. We often carry those mechanisms and use them long after they are needed.

Your job is to be in the now and to release all responses that are no longer relevant to the present.

As you come to be more open and aware of your intuitive instinct and your energetic body, you will come to accept that as you are navigating your way through your life, however you are feeling is valid and correct for you. Once you are able to see an emotional response, a trigger, for what it truly is, you can work through the trigger and release the emotional response, setting you free from conditions and false self-labeling.

When you are dealing with triggers, remember that they are there for a reason. Triggers present themselves because your soul has undoubtedly had issues with this in the past. Through receiving healing work, you will feel better and notice less of an emotional response to triggers.

Life continues to evolve and we evolve with it. It gets better and better, stronger and stronger. The evolutionary process goes through physical, emotional, and spiritual refining so it can return back to itself, so it can know itself as itself, which is universal Source energy.

All cultures have healers and persons of faith who, through ritual and intention, clear the path of energy flow for healing to occur. Acupuncture is this style of healing, clearing the meridians of stuck "chi" (life force energy), allowing the flow of healing energy to move through the body.

An energy healer blasts open locks, allowing for the release of toxins that have been stored in the body. Those areas are open to be flushed and cleansed with healing energy, the energy of unconditional love. Think of an infected finger in which pus has accumulated under the skin. The skin becomes red, hot, and painful to touch. The pus must be released for the finger to heal. If the pus is not released, the infection will move through the body, creating more disease, and even death.

The same thing happens with stuck energy. Energetic pus in the form of negative self-labeling, false beliefs about the self, false conditions believed to be true, lack of self-love, and lack of self-acceptance, prevent the flow of healthy life force energy, the body's natural ability to heal itself. Energy healing releases the energetic pus, allowing the body to return to a state of harmony, balance, and flow.

Energy healers work on the level of the soul. The soul knows who it is and what it has come to do. The soul comes to Earth, incarnating in a physical body to have experiences. A soul might choose to experience trauma in order to create challenges for it to overcome, to reclaim power, to understand the self, and/or to expand knowledge of experiences. Depending on how much karma the soul has accrued over lifetimes and the more challenging the past life experiences have been, the harder present-day goals are to achieve. Some souls have had very painful and challenging experiences, like living a life of addiction or living in times of war. These souls carry the impact of those lifetimes. Those traumas can be healed and released in the present lifetime, freeing the soul to continue on to new experiences. A person does not need to have conscious recall of trauma in order to manifest present-day symptoms, nor does a person need to be consciously and cognitively aware of trauma for energy healing to occur.

Your intuitive instinct is your direct line communication to Creator energy. As you become more comfortable using your intuitive instinct you will be able to answer the call to Light Workers with confidence, focused intention, and joy.

Glossary
Words You Need to Know

Aura or auric field - energetic bodies around the physical body that protect, filter, regulate, and help to heal the etheric body.

Chakra - wheel of spinning energy radiating out in all directions from specific points along the main meridian line of the body. Lots more on chakras in Chapter 3.

Cord - an energetic connection between two people.

Crystal children - children being born with a highly activated crown (seventh) chakra.

Energy - action behind the communication between atomic and subatomic particles and the impulses that travel, creating communication between the particles.

Energy healer - a being with a greater understanding of energetic patterns who has learned to smooth, heal, and redirect energy to its more highly functional resonance/vibration.

Grounding - energetic, visual connection of a person to Earth, allowing the person to use Earth energy to clear the energy field, calming, centering, relaxing, and empowering.

Grounding cord - the energetic connection that attaches you to Earth, like an umbilical cord, feeding you and connecting you to the healing energy of Earth.

Higher Self - a conscious understanding, through heightened levels of awareness, of the part of the soul that stays behind during incarnation. This incarnate part of the soul has knowledge beneficial to the incarnated self and has deep investment in the growth of the human.

Indigo children - children being born with an activated sixth chakra.

Intuitive Instinct - natural, inherent tendency to follow one's higher guidance.

Light worker - a being who has chosen to stay within the energetic veil to expand awareness, heal, bring light, and have a closer connection to Earth and the energy of love. This understanding aligns with the consciousness of Earth to usher in the enlightened Golden Age. Light workers come to Earth during times of significant shift, maintaining positive consciousness during the transition, assisting all beings.

Soul - a mass of energy within which exists everlasting life-giving essence of Source energy. The soul acts as Source's receptor to experience creation. Source energy is within the soul. As the soul feels, so does Source. The core essence of each soul is the same. The rest of the soul develops as the soul experiences the variety of planes of existence.

About the Authors

John Corsa is a multi-disciplined energy healer and crystologist. In his private practice John provides individual and group healings, presentations, classes and mentoring programs.

Cindy Morris, msw, is a professional counselor and astrologer. She is an author, teacher, presenter and humorist. Her book, *Priestess Entrepreneur: Success in an Inside Job*, has helped many women claim their power in business and the business of life.

Cindy and John have co-authored the channeled LOVE Books: *A Time for Love*, *The Loved and Cherished Heart: Awakening Self-Love*, and *The Traveler's Guide to Love*.

They are the creators of *Reclaim Your Intuition*, a 6-part audio course.

John and Cindy collaborate in writings, teachings, and presentations, opening hearts and minds across the globe to the One Heart Consciousness and the limitless potential for healing and personal evolution.